THE
LITTLE BIRD
ON YOUR SHOULDER

Tapping Into Your Intuition To Get The Answers You Need Fast

KATHARINE C. GIOVANNI

THE LITTLE BIRD ON YOUR SHOULDER
Tapping Into Your Intuition To Get The Answers You Need Fast
Published by:
NewRoad Publishing
A Giowell Group LLC Company
Telephone: 919-263-4003
Email: ron@giowellgroup.com.

First Edition 2021
An application to register this book for cataloging has been submitted to the Library of Congress.

eBook ISBN: 978-1-931109-22-2
Print ISBN: 978-1-931109-21-5

Printed in the United States of America

Cover Design by Angie Alaya

This book is dedicated to you.

YOU GOT THIS!

OTHER BOOKS

By Katharine Giovanni

- Rainbows and Banana Peels
- The Concierge Manual
- Going Above and Beyond
- God, Is That You?
- 101 Great Ways to Improve Your Life: Volume 3 *(Contributing Author)*
- Inspiring Hope

  (Contributing Author)

DISCLAIMERS AND LEGAL NOTICES

The information provided in this book is designed to provide helpful information on the subjects discussed. This book is not meant to be used, nor should it be used, to diagnose or treat any medical condition. For diagnosis or treatment of any medical problem, please consult your physician. The author and NewRoad Publishing are not responsible for any specific health needs that may require medical supervision and are not liable for any damages or negative consequences from any treatment, action, application or preparation to any person reading or following the information in this book. References are provided for informational purposes only and do not constitute endorsement of any websites or sources. Readers should be aware that the websites in this book may change.

Information Accuracy

The author and NewRoad Publishing make every effort to ensure that all information presented in this book is correct. However, we do not guarantee the accuracy of the information contained in this book, and reliance on information provided in this book is solely at your own risk. Every effort has been made to make this book as complete as possible; however, it may yet contain mistakes, both typographical and substantive. Therefore, this book should be used only as a general guide.

Disclaimer of Warranties

This book is provided solely on an "as-is" basis, and the use of the information contained herein is at your sole risk. Except to the extent required by any mandatory applicable law, this book and the information contained herein are not subject to any warranty or condition, express or implied, including, without limitation, any warranty of merchantability, satisfactory quality, fitness for a particular purpose or use, or non-infringement.

Neither the author nor NewRoad Publishing guarantees the accuracy or completeness of any information contained in this book. Neither the author nor NewRoad Publishing assumes any liability or responsibility for any errors or omissions in the information contained in the book. Neither the author nor NewRoad Publishing makes any representations or warranties of any kind, express or implied, as to the book or the information contained herein or the results that may be obtained from the use of information contained in the book. The book and the information contained therein are not, and should not be considered to be, presenting you with any type of business opportunity offering or its equivalent.

Limitation of Liability

Neither the author nor NewRoad Publishing shall be liable for any damages of any kind arising from or in connection with the use of the book or the information contained therein, including, without limitation, mistakes, omissions, errors, or defects, even if the author or NewRoad Publishing is expressly advised of the possibility of such damages. This is a comprehensive limitation of liability that applies to all damages of any kind, including compensatory, direct, indirect, punitive, special, incidental or consequential damages (including but not limited to damages for lost profits or loss of revenue).

Take the chance.
Make the leap.
You got this!

TABLE OF CONTENTS

FOREWORD

BY DR. KATIE NALL

Everyone looks for a silver bullet at some point in our lives. A quick fix. Simple answers to puzzling questions.

Feeling ill? Take this pill.

Not getting along with someone? Just move along.

Not enough money? Work harder!

What happens if you found the silver bullet to <u>all</u> your questions? The one bullet of the BEST advice all the time? What if that bullet was immediately accessible all the time? What if someone shared where to find your silver bullet within a day? Would you be interested? Who wouldn't?

The book you are holding in your hand will tell you where your silver bullet is located, who it is, and how to access it.

Katharine shares methods, techniques, and more importantly deep secrets of her life with you to help you understand how to find, listen, and exercise the little bird on your shoulder. You see, Katharine found this little bird on her shoulder years ago and kept her secret to protect both her bird and Katharine from skeptical birdwatchers – you know, those people who don't listen to their little bird on their shoulder.

But she is sharing all her secrets with YOU – because her little birdie told her YOU are special, have questions, and have been looking for this book. That you have been yearning for a silver bullet to answer your question.

Katharine's life experiences and conversational writing style makes this little book a powerful force for you. She has been where you are today. She has moved beyond and looking back, is reaching out to YOU to beckon you forward to your best life – to become an expert birdwatcher.

And you, my friend, are here. By no coincidence.

There's a reason for you to be holding this book.

You might say a little bird on your shoulder gave you this book. Don't aim your silver bullet at your little bird. Use your little bird *as* your silver bullet.

All you have to do is read this book – maybe like me – more than once, to find your silver bullet.

INTRODUCTION

Have you ever reached a crossroad in your life? A fork in the road?

It's an interesting place actually.

The road on the right is the path that you have been walking all your life.

It's easy. It's familiar.

It's also making you extremely unhappy. It doesn't matter what topic we're talking about here. It could be about your career, relationships, health, or money. The fact of the matter is that you yearn for change.

Plus, you can't ignore the fact that huge potholes have appeared on the road!

You've tried ignoring them but somehow always manage to fall flat on your face whenever you come across one. It's like walking through a field of banana peels! The minute you stand up, you slip on another one, and back down you go.

Now you're simply doing the best you can to walk around them when they appear in front of you.

That's not working too well either.

So here you sit. At a fork in the road. Pondering what to do next.

Since ignoring the potholes hasn't worked very well, and walking around them is hit-or-miss, your intuition tells you to take the road on the left when you reach a fork in the road.

This was me in 2014.

I clearly saw both roads in front of me. The one on the right was filled with the work I had been doing for over 20 years. The one on the left was more spiritual in nature and would allow me to openly use the intuitive abilities I was born with.

I could hear my Inner Voice urging me to the left.

So why did I not leap on it with gusto you ask?

I had too many questions.

What if it doesn't work?

What if it's a dead end?

What if it doesn't make money and we can't pay our bills?

I was still in treatment for breast cancer and money was an issue. Our medical bills were seriously out of control.

I had no answers at the time. All I could see was an empty road in front of me. The familiar one was still there on my right. Its only allure was that I knew that road. Sure it was hard and filled with potholes, but it was familiar to me. Good, bad, or ugly, I was used to it.

The one on the left?

No idea.

So instead of taking it, I just ignored it and continued walking on the more familiar path.

Over the years I thought about trying the new road, but various people talked me out of it. They advised me to stay on the "right" road. So I decided to write an inspirational book about my cancer journey. Maybe THAT would stop the road from appearing in front of me all the time.

Nope.

Although the book did well, it didn't stop the darn road from appearing.

Then one day out of the blue, I made a new friend on Facebook. We talked on the phone for hours and really got to know each other. We felt like sisters who had known each other forever.

A few weeks later, my new friend joined me at my fork in the road.

As Katie sat down, she clearly saw both roads in front of me, and immediately pushed me to take the road on the left.

The one I had been hiding from for years.

I smiled at her politely but didn't get up.

She smiled politely back and urged me to the left again.

I expertly changed the subject.

Katie expertly changed the subject right back.

She then settled herself even deeper in the ground next to me unwilling to give up.

A few weeks later, Katie suggested that I join her Mastermind group filled with like-minded people.

It was wonderful. I loved these people! Still do.

A few weeks later, my new friends joined me at my fork in the road.

After they sat down, they politely listened to my reasons for not taking the new path. Then they urged me to take the new road.

All. Of. Them.

Sigh.

I valiantly tried to change the subject, but they all ignored me and continued to urge me forward.

I still didn't get up, but I was wavering.

My new friends stubbornly didn't move. They just kept lovingly urging me forward.

Then an email arrived.

It was one of my favorite inspirational newsletters written by a friend of mine. By now I am sure you are not surprised that it was all about listening to your Inner Voice and how the world needs you.

Coincidence?

I actually don't believe in them. I never have.

It was the little bird on my shoulder ... my Inner Voice urging me forward.

A voice I have heard all my life.

A voice that has literally saved my life.

The year was now 2021 and it was time.

With my soul friends and family firmly by my side, I got up, dusted myself off, took a deep breath, and began to gingerly walk down the road.

You know the one.

The one on the left.

TWO beautiful women named Katie helped me to finally take the new path. Thanks are just not enough. Sending you both love.

1.   I was listening to music on Spotify while I was writing this chapter. Katy Perry's song "Bigger Than Me" played twice! If you haven't heard the song, listen carefully to the lyrics as she sings. Thank you so much Katy. Message received.

2.   To reach my good friend Dr. Katie Nall, who offers all sorts of fantastic services to help you, and who wrote the foreword to this book, please visit www.NallEdgeCo.com. She is the real deal. Trust me.

CHAPTER 1

As I was writing this book, the Champlain Towers South building in Miami collapsed killing hundreds of people.

One of the survivors is alive today because she listened to her intuition.

According to a story on CNN, the night before the collapse, Iliana put her medications and her credit cards in her purse. She also didn't take her sleeping pill.

She woke up around 1:00 am by what she called a "rare force." When she walked into the living room, she immediately saw a crack on the ceiling that was moving down the wall fast.

A "force inside her" told her "You have to run to save your life."

So she ran.

She is one of the few survivors.

What happened? What did she hear? Where did it come from?

Have you ever heard a voice in your mind that tells you something that saves your life?

Many people around the world hear or feel something deep inside of them that turns into life-saving information.

Are they special people or can we all do this?

We all do this.

Every day.

It's your intuition speaking to you.

My friend Meshele had this happen to her once. After a seriously long day, she was exhausted and fell asleep while driving her car down the highway. She woke up when she "heard" someone yell her name. She had just enough time to swerve away from the guard rail, which would have killed her on impact.

These two stories are not unique. Millions of people all over the world have heard this "inside force." Listening to their intuition literally saved their life.

Personally, my intuition, which I lovingly call the little bird on my shoulder, has saved my life three times.

Not that I am counting of course.

~ ~ ~

(If you wish to read CNN's story, the link is in the bibliography at the end of this book.)

CHAPTER 2

FINDING MY WAY OUT OF THE DARK

The first time was in 1974 when my parents divorced. Not your usual quiet divorce mind you, but a loud, angry, in-your-face one. So angry they sued each other, which meant I had to testify in court. It was horrible.

I was 13.

Now combine this with the fact that I was being bullied in school on a regular basis and you get an angry, dark, and sad teenager with bad self-esteem and a serious attitude.

The stress was crippling.

After the court hearing was over, I remember spending the next few weeks slipping into the depths of depression. I fell deep into the abyss. I slept all the time, was angry at everyone, and didn't eat.

One day after a particularly horrible day at school I decided that I had had enough. I wanted it all to stop! So I started to think that maybe, just maybe, it would be easier on everyone if I just left the planet. Besides, who would miss me if I committed suicide? My parents were always fighting, and I didn't think that anyone at school would really care since I was always getting bullied. I had a few good friends, and my brother who I loved dearly, but I really thought they would all get over it quickly after I was gone.

At least that's what I thought at the time.

That night after dinner, I went to my mother's room and quietly grabbed her bottle of aspirin. I sat down at my desk and emptied the entire bottle. For the next few minutes I methodically lined dozens of pills into several rows on the desk.

I stared at them for a long time.

Instead of taking them, however, an Inner Voice I didn't know I had urged me to call the one person on the planet that got me - my best friend Vivienne. I thought it was odd at the time because the Voice sounded just like my own. So I shook it off and tried to ignore it. Didn't work though because the Voice kept whispering her name over and over in my head. So to make the Voice stop, I eventually got up from my desk, went to the hall telephone (*remember it was 1974 technology*), dialed her number, and pulled the long cord into my room so we could talk in private.

She listened to me patiently while I explained what I was doing. All the feelings I had stuffed inside my body for months came pouring out.

When I finished, she spent the next 20 minutes talking me out of it.

After our call, I scooped up all the pills and put them back into the bottle. I raced down the stairs, threw the bottle of aspirin onto my mother's bed, and grabbed my jacket. I remember briefly stopping to ask my mother if I could spend the night at Vivienne's. When she said yes, I raced out of the house and ran all the way there arriving in record time. We talked well into the night, and I woke up feeling better than I had in weeks.

Eventually I came to realize that suicide was a permanent solution to a temporary problem.

And Vivienne? Although I was the first life she saved, she became a vascular surgeon and went on to save hundreds of lives.

And yes, we are still good friends to this day.

If you are depressed, or feeling like you want it all to end, please reach out to a friend like I did. Or you can call the national suicide hotline at 800-273-8255. Kindest people in the world.

You can also visit https://suicidepreventionlifeline.org/.

You are a beautiful soul with a shining light! Your life has purpose! You might not believe it right now, but it does.

Beauty CAN come out of the ashes.

CHAPTER 3

For the next few decades, I ignored my Inner Voice. Why? I was busy finishing up school and starting my career. I got even busier when I married and had two sons.

I also didn't tell anyone that I had conversations with my Inner Voice.

Not. One. Person.

Why you ask?

When I was in my teens and twenties, society shunned people with abilities like mine. We were labeled as crazy and were accused of practicing hoo-doo-voo-doo. Since I was bullied on a regular basis in grammar school, I decided early on to hide my skills so I would fit in. I wanted to be like everyone else.

It was the same with my birth family. I was considered the rebel, the one who was different. So to be more "normal" I just never talked about it and desperately tried to fit in.

Since I never turned my Inner Voice off completely, I felt quiet nudges over the years, but for the most part I just ignored it.

Until I couldn't.

It was the fall of 1996 when the little bird on my shoulder decided it was tired of being ignored.

My husband and I were watching television when I suddenly got the feeling that I was being "watched." I turned my head and saw an angel standing in the doorway outside the bedroom. She was wearing a brocade gown with long ribbons running through the bodice. She smiled at me, and then in the time it takes to blink an eye, she was gone.

For two weeks, I didn't tell anyone about the angel because I wasn't sure that I really saw her. Still, the image stayed with me. I would find myself remembering it at various times during the day until I knew that it was real.

The little bird on my shoulder wanted me to stop ignoring it. So I stopped rejecting it and started to pay attention again.

I also decided to finally tell someone.

My husband was the very first person on the planet to hear about both the angel I saw, and the fact that I could have conversations with my Inner Voice, and no, he didn't fit me for a straight jacket. He did say that he thought everyone has some sort of intuitive ability, a gut-feeling that we don't always trust. Today we share our intuitive connections with each other all the time, so if he commits me, our sons will have to commit him too!

After that night, I spoke to the little bird, my Inner Voice, on a regular basis. It guided me, soothed me, and pointed me in the direction I should go.

It was my best friend. My guide through life. I trusted it completely.

In 1998, the little bird on my shoulder quietly became my business advisor and led me the entire way. I learned to trust it completely as its wise advice led me to start a concierge business that same year. It later advised me to write a book about the industry, which is how I became one of the original Founders of the Independent Concierge Industry.

Although I listened to the little bird every day, I still didn't tell anyone outside of my inner circle of friends and family. Especially when it came to my concierge consulting business. I would choose my words carefully when my Inner Voice came through with guidance for someone I was speaking to. People would often ask "how do you know that?" and my normal answer would be something like "just a feeling," or "years of experience."

I never told them what had really happened.

That my Inner Voice had gently whispered the words to me in my mind.

I would "hear" an answer, "see" an image in my mind, or just "know" the answer. Sometimes all three at once. I became an expert at quickly translating the guidance I received into everyday language for the person I was speaking to.

In 2002, I took a deep breath and decided to write a book about it. Strangely, the book didn't do very well and went out of print shortly after. Although this depressed me, I shook it off and kept moving forward.

As the years rolled by, I wrote more books on various subjects. With two sons, dogs, and our concierge consulting business, life was busy.

CHAPTER 4

The little bird saved my life again in 2012. I would seriously be dead right now if I hadn't listened to it.

It was February 2012.

Although it was always nudging me in various directions, on this particular day it was louder than usual.

"You should start jogging."

Not a banner moment for most of you, but for me? I had been allergic to exercise of any form all my life. Although I tried my best to ignore it, I simply couldn't get the words out of my head. The fact that my Inner Voice literally shouted the words at me made me pay attention more than usual. So using the Couch-to-5K® Running Plan, I began to run.

About six weeks later I was down from a size 14 to an 8. I desperately tried to ignore the fact that the weight was melting off me faster than normal. Deep down I knew it wasn't normal.

The day before my birthday, I did a breast self-check. Something I do each year. This time I found a lump.

A few days later, I was at the doctor's office. After examining me she immediately sent me out for tests. The fact that she literally RAN out of the exam room to make the arrangements wasn't lost on me. I knew it was bad.

I had Stage 3 Triple Positive Breast Cancer, and it was growing lightning fast.

To make a long story short, I was in surgery a few weeks later and was sick for two years, four if you count all the surgeries. I had to have ten operations including a double mastectomy, chemotherapy, and radiation. It was a horrible journey through what felt like a sea of banana peels that I was constantly slipping on. Eventually, I won the war and became cancer free.

Here's the kicker.

My surgeon told me that if I hadn't lost all that weight, I would be dead as the lump was in a very strange place. To make matters worse, the doctors told me that I fell into the 10% of women whose breasts were so dense that mammograms didn't work. Wish I had known THAT when I was younger!

So if I hadn't listened to my Inner Voice and lost all that weight, we wouldn't be talking to each other right now because I would be dead. I would have left with the grim reaper when he visited me.

The little bird had saved my life for the second time.

Katharine C. Giovanni

For those interested in reading more about my journey through breast cancer and the first half of my life, you can pick up my award-winning inspirational book "Rainbows and Banana Peels."

Available on all my websites including, www.katharinegiovanni.com, www.guidedtalk.com and Amazon.

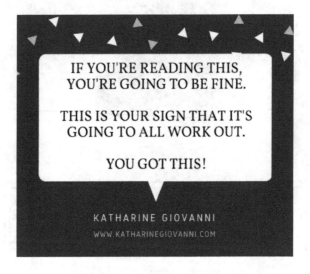

CHAPTER 5

In 2020, the little bird saved my life for the third time. This time I was with my dog.

Almost every day I take my little dog out for an afternoon walk down to the traffic circle and back. Since this particular day was so sunny and beautiful, we took our time so that we could both enjoy the sun. I had spent the day writing in my office and needed the break.

As we reached the halfway point around the circle, I randomly decided to double back and walk back the way we had come.

As I started to cross the street, the little bird yelled at me...

"She is not going to stop!"

Although I was already halfway through the intersection, I stopped dead in my tracks. By this time I knew to listen to it without hesitation. Seconds later, a car ran through the stop sign and blew right past me. She stopped a few yards from me after realizing what she had almost done. She then opened her window, waved at me, and then kept going into our neighborhood.

If I hadn't listened to the little bird on my shoulder and stopped right then and there, my dog and I would be dead because she was driving so fast.

CHAPTER 6

Three times I almost died.

Three times I was saved by listening to the little bird on my shoulder, that Inner Voice we all have.

Your inner force.

It's like the Law of Gravity. This law works whether you believe in it or not.

In fact, you can call it anything you like, and it will still work.

How about calling it the Law of Staying on the Ground?

Doesn't matter. Still works.

Oh you don't believe in the Law of Gravity?

Still doesn't matter. Still works.

Your Inner Voice is the same.

It's going to work regardless of whether you believe in it or not.

You can call the Voice anything you like. You can call it the little bird on your shoulder, a gut feeling, hunch, your Intuition, Inner Voice, Higher Self, The Source, The Presence, or you can call it God, Angels, Guides, Jesus, Allah, or the Universe.

Whatever makes you feel the most comfortable is fine.

There are thousands of names for it in the world right now. In fact, out of curiosity I searched the internet and found an article that listed 950 names!

Just like the Law of Gravity, however, it doesn't matter what you call it.

In fact it doesn't care. Still works.

Even if you don't believe in it, you will **still** get messages in various forms to help you.

The energy is inside of you and it's real.

It's your higher self. Your intuition. Your Inner Voice. Your gut. Your heart.

It's the little bird on your shoulder.

It not only knows the direction you should be going, but it knows where all the potholes are and will help you avoid them if you let it.

You were never meant to go through life without help.

For example, your "gut" will suddenly tell you to not turn onto that road. Even though you turn down that road every single day! It urges you to take another road home.

It gives you a bad "feeling" that makes you stay away from something or someone, or it makes you want to leave somewhere immediately. You don't know why; you just know that it feels wrong somehow.

Or, your little bird will make you "feel" like you should call up a loved one. They pass away a few hours after your call.

That's the little bird on your shoulder. It's your intuition singing at you.

My goal for this book is to show you how to talk to the little bird on YOUR_shoulder so you can have your own guided talks and get the answers you've been searching for.

This book is not meant to be a complete and full guide. It's merely here to get you started on your journey.

As I was writing the last chapter, Coldplay's song "Higher Power" came on.

Coincidence?

I don't believe in them.

You can't make this stuff up.

As I've said many times, pay attention to everything around you including the music playing.

How do you know when it's a message?

Trust me. You'll know. The little bird on your shoulder will tell you.

CHAPTER 7

HOW YOU GET YOUR ANSWERS

Why don't you hear your Inner Voice? Perhaps because you talk to it using a different method than I do.

There are a bunch of ways people listen to the little bird on their shoulder. In fact I recently found an article that listed ten! For the purposes of this book, however, I'm only going to talk about the four most common. Although there are other less common ways such as touch, smell, and taste, I'm limiting the discussion to the four main senses.

Hear

Like me, many people **hear** their intuition. The formal name is clairaudience, and literally means "clear hearing." Most of the time, the messages I receive sound just like my own voice in my head. I also get messages via music and sounds.

See

Other people **see** the answers. The formal name here is Clairvoyance and means "clear seeing." People see images in their minds, and sometimes can "see" spirits in the room with them. Can you "see" your childhood bedroom in your mind right now? Can you see the color of the walls? That's clairvoyance.

Feel

Some people **feel** their intuition. It's called Clairsentience and means "clear sensation or feeling." Have you ever walked into a room and it just feels wrong? Or you've walked in, and it feels fantastic? It just makes you happy! Or perhaps you shake someone's hand and get a bad vibe from them? A feeling you just can't shake no matter how hard you try. That's clairsentience. You physically feel it.

I think it goes without saying here, that if you walk into a room and it feels "off" you should probably leave. Make sure you look around and see who is around you and where you are. Also, you might consider writing about the experience in a journal when things like this happen. When this happens to me, I will often email myself so I can keep a record of it. I'll then download it to a file on my computer.

Trust the little bird on your shoulder.

Empaths

Another one in the "feeling" category are the empaths. Also called clairempathy. These people sense the feelings of other people (*and often spirits*). It means clear emotion. They can physically tune into the emotions of other people, animals, and places.

Without proper training, however, empaths can get quite sick as they're literally taking other people's "stuff" into their own body. If this is you, I have some great exercises in the back of this book that will help. Pay special attention to the "bubble" exercise. I also suggest you google "empaths" as you'll find tons of articles and people to assist you.

Know

Ever just **know** something? One minute you don't and the next minute the information you needed is in your brain? A sudden idea or thought that is always 100% spot on? That's Claircognizance and means "clear knowing." Ever get asked a question and you immediately answer, and then wonder where THAT came from? That's clear knowing.

Want to read more on this topic?

Just do a search on the words "clair senses" and you'll find all sorts of books, articles and videos.

If you hang out
with me for too
long I'll brainwash
you into believing
in yourself.

YOU GOT THIS!

www.KatharineGiovanni.com

CHAPTER 8

Most of us live from the neck up. We're taught to think things through. We are more than that. Our intuition is the operating system that connects our heart to our brain. It gives us access to more information than what is inside our mind. It helps us navigate life. "

It's your soul voice.

Your heart song.

You <u>ARE</u> getting intuitive information, perhaps you are just not aware of it.

How about the times that a thought or name just flies into your mind at EXACTLY the right time? That's your intuition. It's the little bird on your shoulder gently whispering to you. Or you read the lyrics to a song, and it immediately sings to your soul. Those are messages designed to help you.

Of course, you could be suppressing or blocking the messages.

Here's an example.

Something inside of you is screaming. Screaming that you are in the wrong place, have the wrong idea, or are with the wrong person.

You ignore it of course. Just stress you tell yourself. You're being ridiculous right? So you continue moving forward because even though it feels wrong, it looks fine to you.

You block it. No logical reason to believe a feeling, right?

Wrong.

Before you know it everything turns out bad. The crap hits the fan and you're knee deep in it.

Turns out your feeling about it was correct all along.

That was your gut. Your intuition. Your Inner Voice. Your higher self.

The little bird on your shoulder.

Blocks

When you read the word "block" just now, what popped into your mind? Anything or nothing?

If it was a specific memory, person, word, or color, then I suggest you stop reading for a bit and try and focus on that right now. It could be the source of your block. Sit with it for a few minutes and see what comes up for you. If nothing comes up, I have exercises at the end of this book designed to help you.

Go ahead. I can wait. I'll be right here when you get back.

Another reason you might be blocked is emotional. If you are REALLY attached to a particular outcome, and you want it with all your heart and soul, then those thoughts might suppress the answers, or turn it off completely.

So what can you do?

Often the little bird on your shoulder is the quietest voice. That small voice in the back of your mind that whispers the answer to you. The answer might be in the next picture you see on the internet, or an article that catches your eye. If you are not paying attention, however, you might miss it.

So how do you get the information?

As I said in an earlier chapter, you'll see, hear, feel, or know the answer. We are all unique with our own way of tapping into our intuition.

That being said, please don't try and "think" your way to a solution. It won't work. Trust me, I've tried. The solutions that come out of my brain might get me there eventually, but they're never quite right and the road is often rough. When I attach my heart to the problem, the solutions that come out sing to me like a beautiful song. Things flow.

Just "be" with the problem for a while. I suggest that you go for a walk and concentrate on the nature around you so that you can stop thinking about it. Or go into another room and just sit quietly for a few minutes. Let it float in your brain for a while. Stop trying to force an answer to come. If you let go and allow your intuition to work its magic, the answer will come to you.

I often have to do this. When an answer doesn't come, I will often just sit with the problem for a bit. I need to just "be" for a few minutes so the answer can come into my mind.

Let me give you an example.

(The following story goes into the "some clients you never forget" category.)

Twelve years ago, I was conducting a two-day private training session with a client who had purchased a lobby concierge company from her boss. For those who don't know, this is a company who puts concierge in the lobby of a residential or office building. In this case, it was a condominium.

When we got to the fee setting part of the day, I asked her how the company was doing.

"Horrible. We're not making a profit at all."

"How did your boss do before you purchased the company?" I inquired.

"She was losing money left and right, and about to go bankrupt. That's why she sold it to me. I got it for a really cheap price!"

"I'm sure you did." I replied smiling. "How much are you charging each customer?"

"$5.00." she answered simply.

"For what?" I asked.

"For anything" she replied.

"Even if it's something that takes an hour to do?" I asked in disbelief.

"Yes. For everything" she replied.

Easy fix, I thought to myself.

"Well, we'll simply raise your prices."

"I can't do that" she answered. "The residents in the building won't pay anything higher as they're all used to that price. Their Homeowner Association would never approve it and I will lose the only building I have!"

"Well, if you keep charging that low a price point, you'll be out of business soon."

"Yes I know. That's why I am here. I was hoping you would help me figure out what to do."

"You absolutely don't want to raise your fees?"

"No" she replied.

"Why not go out and get another client? Plenty of residential buildings in your city."

"I don't have the time." She replied. You could see the look of desperation in her eyes.

Remember it was 2008 and we were in a recession, so marketing a business that most people had never heard of was tough. Even harder for someone like my client who was very young and new to the concierge industry.

I was banging my head against the table at this point. She honestly believed that she would lose the contract with that building if she raised the prices on them. She was adamant about it and simply wouldn't budge.

After a few minutes of trying to convince her to raise her prices, or do some marketing to get a second building, I decided to give us both a 10-minute break. Mostly because I needed a few minutes to let the problem sit in my head so my Inner Voice could give me an answer that would work for her. Walking away for a few minutes allowed my mind to quiet down so that I could "hear" the answer.

When I came back, I had the answer!

"Why don't you charge $5.00 for every 15 minutes of service, as long as it's within a certain distance from the building? Outside of that service area, you charge more. If it's a service you need to get into a car to do, then you raise it even more. We can talk about Zone pricing and packages residents can purchase. Would that work?"

She loved it!

For the next hour, we worked on the exact numbers and some packages she could offer. She was thrilled! The residents and their homeowner's association still saw $5 for each service, and she got to raise the prices. Win-win! She was still earning bird seed, but at least there was a bit more of it.

You see, the answers are there for you. Sometimes you just have to walk away and clear your mind so the answer can flow to you.

CHAPTER 9

THE WALL

I can hear your thoughts as you read this.

You're agreeing with me that intuition works, but yours only works some of the time. The big problem is that you've hit a wall and no matter what you do, you just can't get past it.

You're stuck.

Listen, I totally understand you've hit a wall. I get it. I've hit them too. The problem here is that you are going back to that same darn wall again and again thinking that today will be the day that you finally break through it! It's all you can think and talk about. Getting through that wall has taken over your life! It's all you want to do at this point.

Get out that sledgehammer!

Let's spend an insane amount of time breaking though that wall. We'll read articles, books, visit websites, and watch YouTube videos about how to blast through that wall!

We got this right?

Umm… one question.

Why go through all that work?

Seriously why?

Because someone told you that it takes a lot of "work" to move through your blocks?

Were you taught, like I was, that you have to work hard to get what you want? You have to work hard for a living?

Complete and total rubbish.

Just go around the darn thing.

Seriously. Let the wall be and walk around it.

Give yourself permission to use your intuition to walk around the wall. Remember, you can always go back to the wall to "clear" it. Your Inner Voice will let you know when it's time to circle back and finally break that wall.

For now, just walk around it.

This is called Divergent Thinking.

According to Encyclopedia.com, divergent thinking is "the ability to develop original and unique ideas and to envision multiple solutions to a problem."

That being said, to walk around the wall, I suggest you meditate with a pen and paper on your lap. First, go find somewhere to sit that is different. Someplace different from where you normally sit. Inside, outside, doesn't matter.

Now sit with your questions quietly for a while. The answers will come. Don't force any thoughts, just let thoughts, words and images gently float into your mind. After a few minutes, write down the thoughts and images that you are getting. Do this for a few days in a row and you'll see a pattern emerge.

By the way, if any negative or bad memories or thoughts come up, just say to yourself "that's just a memory" or "that's just a rogue thought" and let it float on. I often say it out loud to the room if I am alone. Although if you are with people, they might look at you weird if you randomly blurt that out! Give it absolutely no emotion and try not to dive into the memory. Take a deep breath, replace it with a positive memory, and keep going.

You can also ask your team of helpers to assist you.

Who am I speaking about?

Are we getting into the hoo-doo-voo-doo part of the book?

Maybe.

<SMILE>

Believe me or not, everyone has a bunch of people on the other side of the veil helping you get through life. Angels, guides, family, friends… bunches of light beings! In fact, every single one of us was born with two guardian angels that stand to the immediate left and right side of your body. They are always there and will remain with you until the day you die. However, they cannot help you without permission. It's one of the Laws of the Universe.

That being said, I have personally given my guardian angels permanent permission to help whenever they like. I'm quite sure they'll need a vacation when my journey on this planet is done, or an aspirin!

So ask for help. Verbally is better. Saying it out loud to the room clearly states your intention, although over the years I have asked for assistance mentally when people are around me.

The assistance will come in the form of a person, an article that catches your eye, a sign on the road, or words you hear in your mind, that sort of thing. Pay attention!

The answers are there for you.

The reason you are reading this little book right now is most likely because you asked for help right?

Don't be afraid of what you can't see. Love is all around you. Help is all around you. All you have to do is reach out and ask.

CHAPTER 10

Yes, you can turn your voice off if you wish. Just set the intention in your mind that you want to turn it off. You can also turn it back on using the same technique.

Although I did ignore it for a while, I never actually turned it off. Why? Honestly, the thought never occurred to me.

Many of us simply ignore our intuition and put our faith in other people. For example, you feel sick and go to the doctor. Your intuition is telling you that something is wrong, but the doctors tell you you're fine and to go home and rest. A few weeks later you end up in the hospital thinking "I knew something was wrong!" I cannot tell you how many times people have said these exact words to me.

Why didn't you trust the feeling? Because you assumed the doctors knew the answer. Sometimes they do, sometimes they don't. They are human after all. You can put your faith in all sorts of people, places, and things instead of looking within and listening to your own inner guidance. People have been doing it for centuries.

Listen, we all have the ability to do this, we just don't believe it. We think that other people do this, but not me. I'm not special.

Rubbish. We are ALL special.

You can do this. You already are. The fact that you are reading this book right now tells me that you are intuitive.

Remember, if you can't shake a feeling in your gut, that strong hunch you sometimes get, then take a long look at it. Go get another opinion from a different professional. Your intuition is that nagging feeling that you just can't shake.

Listen, there is a reason why you can't shake it.

Trust it.

If I hadn't trusted the nagging feeling that I needed to start jogging in 2012, I would be dead right now. Not kidding. Jogging led to weight loss, which in turn allowed me to find a lump in my breast.

If I hadn't listened to the little bird on my shoulder, we wouldn't be having this conversation right now because

I would be dead and having dinner with the grim reaper. So yes, please trust what you hear/feel/see/know.

Plus, since the little bird on my shoulder has saved my life more than once, I think it's best that I don't turn it off.

Might I gently suggest that you leave yours on too?

CHAPTER 11

TRUSTING YOUR INTUITION

Trust.

How exactly DO you trust what your intuition tells you? Especially if you REALLY want a particular outcome.

I won't lie to you. Sometimes it can be hard.

What I can say is that sometimes you just have to have faith that it will all work out.

Easy for me to say? Actually no.

When I got cancer, I clearly wanted a particular outcome. I wanted to live! I also wanted my journey to be as easy as possible. When I went within myself and asked about it, I kept "hearing" that I should trust and all will be well.

Huh? Not exactly a clear answer.

So I asked again.

This time I received the words "Trust the process. You'll be fine."

Weeks passed. Then months. The journey was definitely **NOT** easy. Operations, chemotherapy, radiation, and pain. Lots and lots of pain.

Incredibly hard to hear your Inner Voice when you're on drugs and in pain. So my only recourse was to trust what I had heard at the beginning of the journey. I had to trust that I was doing everything that I could and would indeed "be fine."

I had to trust the process.

As the months dragged on, the drugs I was on prevented me from "hearing" the words my Inner Voice was trying to tell me, but I could still feel them. My gut was telling me to keep going. To not give up. I had a strong hunch that I would get through it.

Sometimes all you have is a feeling to go on. A hunch.

So what did I do?

On days when I was feeling clear, I did some guided writing. In fact, I would ask the same question a few days in a row to see if I got different answers. I never did. I always got the same answers, worded a bit different each day, but basically the same.

When I was really uncertain, I would ask a few intuitive friends of mine what they "got" about whatever question/concern I had at the time. What I found when I did that was that my first "thought" or "feeling" about the problem was often the correct one.

I suggest that you start with the simple questions. Questions and problems that are relatively small and easily solved. Then, when you learn to trust your intuition about the small things, you can work your way up to the big ones.

All that being said, what if you've tried it all and it just doesn't work?

I had a client once who was really trying to start a concierge business. The problem was that everything I told her to do she countered with a "tried that, didn't work" answer. I am stuck, she lamented. What do I do?

So let's talk about that.

What if you can't?

How do you move beyond that?

First, remember that wall of blocks I mentioned earlier in this book? The one you've been trying to blast through?

I'll say it again. Walk around it my friend. Ignore the wall and start fresh. Forgive yourself and give yourself permission to simply move on. You can go back to it later and pull it down. For now, let it be and walk around it.

Remember that journal I suggest you start earlier? Pick it up and write down your dreams and your "hunches" about things. Then, write down what happens. Were you right? Do this for a few weeks.

Soon you'll have written proof that the little bird on your shoulder is spot on with its advice.

Doubt is your enemy here. It's your biggest obstacle. Doubt was the one thing that was holding my client back. She doubted herself. Didn't think she could do it, and she didn't think she deserved it, so she sabotaged it all. She was also addicted to struggling because that's how she grew up.

Life was supposed to be a constant struggle, right?

We must work hard for a living, right?

Total nonsense.

Generational money (and life) struggles can be stopped in their tracks.

By you.

I suggest that you start your new journey from where you are NOW, not from where you were a few minutes ago.

Start fresh right now.

This moment.

Walk around the wall and ignore how it got there and what each brick stands for. Ignore it all. Walk around the wall and shout out to the world "bring it on!

One more thing to remember. The Universe responds to how you FEEL more than the words you say. It's the emotion behind your words that will get you to your destination.

 If you resonate with generational money struggles, then you might try to meditate on the word "tomorrow."

Then, in your journal or on a pad of paper, write down the thoughts, images and words that come to your mind.

I think you'll find some great new things are in store for you!

I listen to loud music when I'm writing. Been doing it since I was a child. Used to drive my parents crazy when I was doing homework! As I was writing this chapter, I was listening to Celine Dion sing the song "Ashes" from the "Deadpool 2" motion picture soundtrack.

The words "let beauty come out of ashes" sang to my soul.

You CAN rise from the ashes.

You got this.

CHAPTER 12

If you look back, I'll bet my last dollar that you can remember one day that completely changed your path forever. I've actually had a few "change-your-life" days over the years that have caused me to pivot, but I will never ever forget that very first one.

It was 1979 and I was 18 years old. I had just graduated from high school and decided to take a year off before I went to college. My dysfunctional childhood had turned me into an angry teenager with no direction.

So that summer, my father sent me away to a teen outward bound program. Mostly to get me out of the hot city, but I think he hoped that it might give me a new perspective on life. Since I had nothing better to do, I agreed and spent the next 3 months in the woods hiking up mountains, canoeing down rivers and generally learning how to survive in nature.

In the middle of the program, we were all required to spend three days alone in the woods. I was given a tent, a ridiculously small bag of granola, and was placed next to a stream. They checked on me a few times a day, but never spoke.

Now something strange happens to you when you are all alone in the woods … you start to think.

The first thing I did was to hang my food up on a tree so the animals wouldn't get to it.

Then I made sure that my tent was up correctly as I didn't want to get wet if it rained, which of course it did later that night. Magically I stayed dry!

Then, with nothing left to do, I started to think and reached for the notebook and pen that I was allowed to bring with me. I instinctively began to write.

As I sat there, the little bird on my shoulder took me back in time, and I examined everything that had happened to me. The memories made me happy, sad, cheerful, and angry. Back and forth it went as the memories flowed through my mind.

Eventually, the garbage that I had been telling myself for years began to sound really stupid. It's hard to lie to yourself when you are alone with only your Inner Voice to keep you company.

By the end of the day, I was finally able to see what I had become, and I didn't like her at all. She was a spoiled angry brat who was given a hard start in life, but had a lot going for her in spite of it. I remember crying for what seemed like hours. Then once I stopped feeling sorry for myself, I became angry. I stomped around the woods for a while throwing sticks and rocks and yelled at the air around me.

A few hours later, totally exhausted from the emotion of it all, I found myself on a large boulder by the stream where I had pitched my tent. I can remember watching the sun set behind the mountain I was next to. I then stared at the fish in the stream and poked at the water with a stick to pass the time. My mind was numb, and I felt empty.

I had nowhere to go, no one to talk to, and no destination in mind.

It was just about then that it happened. Even after all these years, I can still remember the exact moment when my entire world changed.

As I looked into the stream, a slow anger started to boil under my skin. It was like my brain snapped. I decided to show everyone how wrong they were about me. I was NOT the lost cause people thought I was.

A fierce determination overtook me and I remember thinking that I would show them all, and prove them all wrong. I was going to become a lighthouse and would be an example of how to do it right.

Once back at base camp, I began helping out everywhere I could. The counselors were stunned and asked me what brought on the change. I just shrugged and told them that I had simply decided to grow up.

I didn't dare tell them what had really happened - that my Inner Voice and I had spent hours talking to each other. The conversations caused me to have an epiphany, an "ah ha" moment.

It quite literally changed my life.

Unfortunately, it took another 15 years before I was finally able to become the teacher that I dreamed about. Why? Mostly because I was young and had a lot to learn, but I'll never forget the moment when it all started.

How about you? Can you remember the day that changed your life?

What if today was another one?

Why not make today the day that changed your life?

No?

Not ready?

Giving up is easy right?

Seriously. It takes no effort at all to just throw in the towel and walk away.

What is not easy is staying the course.

Rolling up your sleeves, taking a deep breath, and diving in is hard right?

I should know, as my breast cancer battle caused me to shut down the company that I started. Walking away was the easy part.

What was NOT easy was starting over and trying again until I got it right. Once I was healthy again, I reformed the company and got back on track.

It would have also been easy to give up on my cancer battle and go up to heaven, but that's not who I am. I'm a fighter who wins her battles.

Giving up is clearly not in my vocabulary.

Here's the reality: If you want to live your dream, then don't give up no matter what! Don't listen to people when they try to talk you out of your dream.

Listen to your Inner Voice instead. The little bird who has been sitting on your shoulder since the day that you were born.

Life has taught me many things, but one of them is this: Your life's path is yours to choose. No one can do it for you. Others can offer advice and comments, but at the end of the day, it's yours to win or lose.

Did you know that studies show that only 10 percent of your success and happiness comes from outside sources? Only 10 percent! So clearly your life and business success is an inside job. It's a head trip. It's all up to you.

It's about trusting that little bird on your shoulder.

Stand up and win.

Stand up and live your dream.

Stand up and never ever give up.

Listen, you haven't reached the end; you have reached the beginning of a brand-new journey.

Your new life starts right now.

"Wherever you've been, and whatever you've done so far, your entire life was building up to this moment. Now is the time to burst forth into your greatness–a greatness you could never have achieved without going through exactly the things you've gone through.

Everything you've experienced was grist for the mill by which you have become who you are. As low as you might have descended, in God there are no limits to how high you can go now.

It is not too late. You are not too old. You are right on time. And you are better than you know."

Marianne Williamson

CHAPTER 13

I have a pet peeve. I just HATE reading a beautiful meditation in a book and then trying to remember all the words so I can do it myself. I always manage to miss something!

That being said, I am recording an audio book so you can listen to the book.

Please visit my websites for more information.

www.KatharineGiovanni.com

www.GuidedTalk.com

Trying to practice mindfulness?

Look at your phone's date and time every time your mind goes to the past. Or every time your mind goes to what you are worried about. This reminds you to be present right now.

(By the way, that "worry" is already in the past)

RIGHT NOW ... in this moment ... as you read this ... all is well. Now breathe that in for a minute or two before you go back to what you were doing.

Katharine Giovanni

www.KatharineGiovanni.com

Guided Writing

In the 1960s, they called going within "meditation." In fact, many still do. I prefer the term "going within" because it is more to the point. You go within yourself to speak to the little bird on your shoulder. Your Inner Voice. Your intuition. Your higher self. Essentially, you are blocking out all outside thought and stimulants and turning inside to your soul or spirit. Here's how it works:

Sit down at your computer and open a fresh document. You can also use a pen and pad of paper.

Put your fingers on the keys (or pick up your pen).

Ask a question. Any question. Ask it either silently in your mind or out loud to the room.

Now, this is important. Write down the very first words or images that come to your mind. Don't hesitate. Just write down the first thoughts that come to your mind whatever they are. It's like that old word association game that we played as children. The one where I say "sky" and you say the first thought that comes to your mind like "blue." I say "black"; you say "white." Same exact thing. If you see an image, feel free to draw it, or describe it in words.

Once you ask your question, immediately write down the very first words or images that form inside of your mind. Do it immediately, and don't hesitate or even think about what you are writing. Simply write down the words or images, whatever they are. Don't think about where the thoughts/images are coming from—because it doesn't matter right now where they are coming from. Just write without thought. Don't question the words that form in your mind, even if you suspect that they are coming from your own mind. Don't go there right now. For now, I simply want you to blindly write them down no matter what they are.

Ask another question, either silently in your mind or out loud to the room.

Again, immediately write down the very first thoughts that come to your mind no matter what they are. I can't stress this enough (so I'll say it again)—write down the first thoughts and words that form in your mind no matter what they are. Blindly write them down. Even if you think that you are answering yourself, that's fine, write them down anyway. Keep writing until your "thoughts" end.

Ask another question and again write down the thoughts that come to mind.

Now go back and reread your answers. A friend of mine did this exercise and I asked her how it went. She told me that some of the answers completely surprised her and were not replies that she would have said to herself.

We were never meant to go through life alone without help. We were meant to chat with our spirit guides and guardian angels. Nothing is out of reach for we can all do this!

When I was a little girl, I can clearly remember having conversations with myself. I would talk and then would hear the answer in my mind. As I got older, I eventually learned that it was the little bird on my shoulder who had been talking with me all along! Once I accepted that, then it all became a little easier.

I also know that many of you might be thinking that this is just a little bit eerie. Sitting at your computer seemingly talking to yourself? Just the thought might be a little unsettling.

I was chatting about this concept with a friend of mine, and I asked her where she thought the answers were coming from. She told me that she figured that the answers were coming from her heart and not her brain. Once she had that thought, the conversations felt natural to her.

The answers are your heart songs. They come from deep within your soul and are your highest thoughts.

How to Clear Your Mind and Focus – Method 1

Having trouble relaxing your mind? Thoughts flowing through it like a freight train? Here's a good meditation that will help.

By the way... meditating is hard for me too. It's hard to quiet down your brain when thoughts of what you "should" be doing race across your mind. So I let the thoughts race by for a few minutes, and then I do the exercise below.

First, choose a time of day when you will be undisturbed for a while. Find a spot in your home where you feel most at peace. Perhaps it's your bedroom, a favorite chair, or that sofa in the den. Or it can be outside. All good.

Now feel the peace around you. Feel the warmth of it surround you like an old sweater. Feel your breath slowly go in and out. Hear the loving silence and know the calmness of it.

Relax your body. Feel yourself become serene and calm. Use your imagination to travel through your body and see your head, neck, arms, stomach, hips, legs, and feet become relaxed.

Feel at peace here—in this spot, in this moment, in this place. You have no worries right now. You have put them on the shelf. You have no problems and no concerns. You are no longer angry or sad about anything. Your thoughts are quiet. The outside world has been left on the outside, just for a moment. You are now inside where it is peaceful, safe, and loving. You have no one to worry about and nothing to do except enjoy the peace and quiet.

All your worldly problems have fallen away. Now stand up and go to your computer or pick up your pen/paper. Keep this feeling of inner peace with you and wrap its essence around you. Type your first question and then begin your guided writing.

The calmer and more relaxed you are, the easier it will be to focus on the words and images from the little bird on your shoulder.

How to Clear Your Mind and Focus – Method 2

Like before, go to the most peaceful place in your home, or outside if that is better for you. Try and pick a time of day when you will not be interrupted for a while.

Now take a deep breath, hold it for a few seconds, and let it out again slowly. Do this three times.

Forget about your life for a moment. Forget about everything you've done today. Forget about everything you did yesterday.

Close your eyes and feel the peace and serenity surround you like a warm bath. Breathe deeply and with each incoming breath feel more peace surround you. Draw it in and feel its love.

Now use your imagination to create a peaceful place. Visualize it in your mind, like a movie playing inside of your mind.

Let me give you an example.

Can you "see" your childhood bedroom in your mind right now?

Can you see the bedspread and the pictures on the walls?

Can you see the whole room in your mind?

That's visualization. You are using your imagination to create your childhood room in your mind.

Now don't worry if you're having trouble, because not everyone can picture what they are thinking about. Some people can't really see the room, but they can feel its presence. They simply know that it is there. If you are having trouble visualizing a peaceful place, just think about the place that you'd like to be in. Think about what you'd like to see in it and where it is. If a picture of it forms in your mind, then great! If not, just think about what it might look like. Say the words out loud if you wish. Create the peaceful place.

Look around you. Are you in a room? Are you outside? Where are you? What does it look like? Is there a spot to sit down? What colors do you see? Create the place in your mind and see everything inside of it. Make it your perfect place, a place where you feel most at peace. You can make it anything you want. Have fun creating this!

Imagine that you are walking around your special place. Feel the earth under your feet and see the colors around you. Suddenly, you notice a big rock in front of you. This rock symbolizes all your worries, doubts, and concerns.

Pick up the rock. Is it heavy? What color is it? See it in your mind. What does it look like?

Now imagine yourself looking to the right. Find some place to place the rock. It's heavy! If you are inside a room, it might be a bookshelf. If you are outside, it might be on a hill or a mountainside.

Place the rock as high up as you can on the shelf, or mountainside, and imagine yourself walking away from it. Don't worry; it will all be there when you get back. You are simply placing it there for safekeeping while you take a little walk.

Relinquish your control over the rock. Remember that it symbolizes the big stuff in your life, the worries, the doubts, the concerns.

It's that wall I was talking about earlier in this book.

Please don't change your mind about it; just change your focus for a moment. Make your focus the here and now. This moment. This place.

Now imagine that you can see a door to the left of the rock. Where did that come from? It wasn't there before! (If you are outside, perhaps it's a path.) Walk toward the door, open it, and walk through.

Open your eyes as soon as you walk through the door. Get up out of your chair and walk over to your computer. With that new door firmly in mind, with the peace and serenity you just found surrounding you, place your fingers on the keyboard of your computer.

You are ready to start. Type in a question. Remember, your doubts and worries are still high up on that shelf or mountainside. Open your mind to the new thought that the little bird on your shoulder is waiting to speak with you. Forget about everything else. Simply know it to be true. Know that the answers that come to your mind are indeed from your Inner Voice.

The Bubble Exercise

Have you ever been in a conversation with someone who has a stomach ache, and strangely your stomach starts to hurt when you walk away?

Or you talk to someone who is angry and then feel angry yourself for no apparent reason?

How about when you walk into a building, and it just "feels" bad. When you leave you are tired and feel sick.

How about the time you spoke to a client on the phone and were incredibly tired after? So tired you had to lie down for a bit.

Many of us are sensitive to the energy around us and can pick up both good and bad vibes from people and places.

If you think you're an empath, then this exercise is critical for you! It will protect your energy so you don't get drained and sick from the people around you.

Have you seen the movie the Wizard of Oz? Remember when Glinda the good witch shows up by floating to the yellow brick road in a giant bubble?

THAT'S what I'm talking about. Here's how it works...

First, imagine a white cord coming from the top of your head (your crown chakra) and it goes all the way up to the heavens. Then, imagine that you are a mighty oak tree with roots that go all the way to the center of the earth.

Now call in your team of helpers. I usually say something like "I call on my team in the highest light." I also call in my team before every session I do with a client.

(As you practice, this becomes easier and faster to do.)

Now imagine that a giant bubble is surrounding you. I always ask my angels to make it the appropriate size, color, and strength.

Now just breath and continue doing what you were doing. If you were about to walk into a building, then do it. You're safely bubbled from whatever energy is in there. If you were talking to someone, you should feel better shortly.

House Clearing Exercise

Speaking of protecting yourself, occasionally negative energy will build up in your home. It comes from many things including the energy from fighting with someone, arguments, depression, anything like that. It can also come from previous owners/tenants alive or dead. I clear my home often by doing the following meditation.

Step 1

Stand up and put your hand on any wall of your home.

Step 2

Close your eyes and bubble yourself using the technique I just shared.

Step 3

Now imagine that you are a tall and proud oak tree with your roots (feet) firmly pressed into the ground. Bare feet are ideal. You could also go outside, in bare feet, and put your hand on the outside of the house so your feet are literally grounded into the soil. If you live in an apartment, all good. You're clearing the entire building! Think about all the souls you're going to help!

Step 4

Now say the following. You can substitute the word "God" with anything you like to make it personal to you.

Thank you God for clearing my home of anything that isn't here for my highest good. Thank you for clearing the people, both seen and unseen, plants, animals, trees, and all the objects inside my home and on the property around it. Thank you for raising my home's vibration to its highest level of light and love. Thank you for clearing and raising the vibration of anything that wasn't here for my highest good. I wish peace, joy, and love to them all. And so it is.

How often should I do this?

When it crosses your mind that you should do it again. Ideally a few times a year.

Do I need to sage my home, play music, use crystals or something?

Only if you want to. If it helps you then go for it. Personally, I don't use them. It's all about intention.

Your Glass of Anger

(This exercise is an excerpt from my book "Rainbows and Banana Peels.")

Pick up a glass and fill it with liquid. It can be any kind of liquid: water, iced tea, soda. Now hold it in front of you with your arm straight out and stay like that for a few minutes.

The glass you are holding represents your anger. The liquid inside the glass represents years and years of fear, resentment, and anger for the things people have done to you. For many of you, it's taken a long time to fill up your glass of anger, and for others the glass was just filled up yesterday.

When I first start getting angry, it's really easy to hold the glass up in front of me. I can balance my life with my anger because it's not affecting where I'm going. I can easily hold it off to the side. It's manageable. However, the longer that I hold this glass, the more my arm is going to tire and eventually hurt.

Soon, my arm is going to really start to ache, and it's going to get harder and harder to hold up the glass. When I first lifted it, I could easily hold it off to the side, but now that my arm is hurting, I can't. In fact, I can't focus on anything but the glass anymore. It's affecting every part of my life now, as the pain is more than I can bear. I'm talking about it to everyone, crying, whining, yelling, screaming, and shouting to everyone who can hear me. I'm also getting resentful about the fact that I have to hold up this darn glass.

The glass of anger has wormed its way into every part of my life now. The longer I hold onto it, the more painful it's going to get. In fact, after a while, I'm going to have to use my other arm to help me hold up the glass.

Now, pay attention to my body language. My life hasn't stopped exactly because I can still sort of see beyond the glass in front of me. That's about it, though, because both my arms are now dedicated to holding up the glass.

If I continue to hold up the glass of anger, and I don't forgive, and I don't put it down, eventually it's going to affect where I'm going because it's going to be right in front of me. The pain is now so intense that the anger is all I can see. I can't hold it off to the side any longer.

If you've decided to keep your anger because you think you can manage it all then great! Skip to the next exercise. Let me warn you though, after a while your little glass of anger is going to turn into a pitcher of anger.

It's going to grow!

The pitcher is worse, of course, because the pitcher of anger that I am holding onto is so big it is now all I can see. I'm now missing opportunities that are being presented to me.

My soul mate might have just walked into the room, but because I'm holding on to the pitcher of anger, I can't see this ideal person and he or she walks away. My dream job, a potential new and fabulous house, a cure for my illness, or a great life-changing opportunity could all appear in front of me, and I won't see them because I'm still focused on the anger, which is now a huge pitcher.

Ideas, things, people, places, none of it's going to happen because all I can focus on is that pitcher of anger I am stubbornly holding on to. My entire life is now focused on the fear, anger, hatred, and resentments that are inside that pitcher.

So what's inside of your glass of anger?

Is the anger stemming from your childhood? From someone in particular? From something someone did or didn't do? Because you are sick, lonely, hungry?

Whatever it is, it is holding you back.

So, how do you get rid of the anger inside the glass?

You already know the answer: forgiveness and gratitude.

It's time. Seriously.

Now, please allow me to be completely clear: Forgiving someone does not mean that they were right, nor does it mean that you want a relationship with them. Forgiving someone means that there is less anger in your glass, and you can finally put the glass down. You might not want to talk to this person, but you've forgiven him or her and you're not resentful and angry anymore. You can finally look at their name on a piece of paper and you don't feel the anger rise up into the back of your throat and choke you.

Now look at your body language. With the glass or pitcher down, you can finally see things around you. Your hands are now free so you can do things. You'll see the opportunities that are flowing to you. Ideas will now flood your brain, and new roads will appear in your path. Why? Because the ideas were trying to flow into your mind, but they were being stopped at the gate because of the anger. You unconsciously pushed the new ideas into the back of your mind because all you could focus on was the anger and resentment inside the glass. You lived it, breathed it, drank it in.

So put down your glass of anger.

It's time, don't you think?

You have suffered enough.

Forgive the people inside the glass.

Who should you start with? The person you are thinking about right now as you read these words.

"You know, Katharine, I HAVE forgiven them!" You might now be saying to me.

Possibly.

Consider this: If you really have completely forgiven them, then why are they entering your mind now as you read these words? Sometimes you have to forgive people more than once. In fact, you might have to do it a bunch of times, especially if the person is family or you live with this person.

"Well, I can't put down my glass of anger and forgive because I'm blocked!"

I hate the word "blocked."

Would you like to know why?

Mostly because the word itself is a block. Just the mere fact that you are telling me you are blocked is a block.

"I am blocked"—possibly the strongest affirmation in the world— is guaranteed to make you stay right where you are. It stops all forward motion because you start to obsess about it. It's all you can think and talk about. You live it and breathe it in every day, searching for that one piece of magical information that will get rid of it.

So you stay blocked because you think you are blocked.

I just hate that word.

Plus, even if you do figure out what it is that has made you angry, you still have that small voice in the back of your mind that wonders if you really did find out what it was because a few months from now you'll find yourself in another dark place and the "block" roller coaster will start all over again.

So here's what I do: I replace the word "block" with "distractions."

What is distracting you from attaining your dreams?

Let's start by writing down what is distracting you right now.

You have work to do for your boss?

You can't get dysfunctional childhood memories out of your head?

Your friends told you that you can't?

You're in a bad relationship?

You have no money in the bank?

You are sick?

Distractions.

I can't put down my glass of anger because I have too many distractions right now and I can't focus on it.

Let's take a look at that last one: You are sick. You are too sick to start moving toward your dream.

Okay, I respect that. Stage 3 breast cancer was a huge distraction for me. Being sick for so many years was horrible. However, I never let my illness prevent me from writing my blog, talking with friends, or consulting with clients— all of which brings me incredible joy. Life is just too darn short to not live in your joy.

So what is distracting you?

Lack of money?

There's a good one!

"I don't have enough money to start."

Okay, fine, your bank account has a $1.50 in it. I get that.

I also understand that the Internet is free, and you can do some research on your dream (or your current distraction) without spending a dime. There is information out there on every topic you can possibly imagine.

What is your heart telling you to do? Your gut? Your Inner Voice?

What was your knee-jerk reaction when I asked what is distracting you?

What was the first thing that popped into your mind?

Start there.

Choose to move forward through your distractions.

Choose to feel the sun on your face, have more than enough money in your bank account, a healthy body, and a happy relationship. Choose this in your mind and then feel the results. Smile about it. Daydream about it. Where would you go if your dream was given to you right now? Daydream about that.

Do that every day.

Think positive, forward-moving thoughts that include loving words such as certain, capable, and happy.

Eventually, people will magically float into your life that will help you get where you want to go, and the negative ones who are holding you back will float out. You will stumble across websites and articles that will inspire you with ideas. You'll see something on television or hear it in a song on the radio. Distractions that took over your life yesterday will disappear today, and you'll be walking in a new direction.

Then you'll be on your way.

So stop saying that you are blocked!

You are not blocked; you are just temporarily distracted.

Your life might look gloomy and miserable now but remember that the sun always comes out after a rainstorm. Hang in there.

Do what I do—when I get into that dark place and random negative situations hit me, I look at the situation as my launching pad to something even greater.

Sure, I was sick for two years, but if I hadn't gone through it, I wouldn't be here with you right now.

After your little glass of anger is empty, bless the energy and then stand your ground. Don't go back and fill up your glass again. Stand your ground! If you can do that, eventually you can use the experience as a launching pad to something even greater. The hurt is a teacher that shows you things about yourself that help you to grow. That's the silver lining. You grow and become greater.

Katharine's Three Levels of Forgiveness

Level 1

You tell them that you forgive them, but you don't really mean it. I forgive you, but I'm not forgetting anything. I remember it all. Your glass of anger is totally full right now; in fact, it's overflowing. What you're really saying is, I know I should forgive you, but I can't because I'm still angry.

Level 2

Now, you have some feeling attached to the words. Your glass of anger is only half-full so you're making progress. You're going to try and forgive because you need to be free. At this stage, "I forgive you" means: Your name still brings up anger, but not as badly as it used to. I can manage it. I really think I have forgiven you, but I can't seem to move on from it. I'm working on it.

Level 3

The words are gone and have been replaced by feeling. Your glass of anger is empty now. Finally, you can say: Although I might not want a relationship with you, I totally forgive you. I can let go and move on now. I am free.

So what do you do right now?

I suggest that you get a mental picture in your mind of the person with whom you are angry.

What are you feeling?

Are you still incredibly angry?

Can you forgive that person?

Do you want to forgive him or her? It's fine if you don't.

What is your heart telling you?

Remember, forgiving someone does not mean he or she was right. It simply means that you are sick and tired of being angry and wish to move on. You want to put down your glass of anger.

There are tons of books and websites on forgiveness and anger that will help you move through this process if you wish more information. You can also try my forgiveness exercise on the next page. You can do this!

Example

I had the hardest time forgiving an old friend of mine. Every time I would see their name, it would bring up the memory and I would get angry all over again.

Why didn't I forgive them?

I did actually. Hundreds of times. It just never stuck.

Why you ask?

Sometimes it comes in layers. Like an onion. You peel off one layer only to find another one beneath it. Over the years, I peeled off many of the layers. I FINALLY was able to let it all go about five years later.

How did I know I had reached level 3 in forgiveness?

I saw their name on Facebook and I had zero emotions around it. Normally, just seeing the name would zing my brain. Now? Nothing. Nada. Zilch.

When you see their name and no emotion comes up, nor do you feel the anger boiling in your stomach, you know you've finally reached that sweet spot of ultimate forgiveness.

The Forgiveness Exercise

Here's how I do it.

I sit in the middle of my bed with all, and I mean ALL my technology off. At the very least, turn the ringer off for a few minutes so that you don't hear it.

Now close your eyes.

Take three deep breaths.

Ground yourself by imagining that a white cord is going from the top of your head all the way up to the heavens. Then imagine that your feet have tree roots on them that go way down to the center of the earth.

Now think about the person you want to start with. Personally, I started with the easy ones first. The girl in grammar school sort of thing. Easy to forgive those right? Work your way up to the hard ones. If you just cannot forgive those hard ones, it's fine. Keep going and circle back to them in a few weeks, months, or years. You'll get there when you're ready. As I wrote earlier, walk around the wall and come back to it later.

See the person in your mind. Remember the circumstances. See it play out in your head like a movie. Don't put any emotion into it as it's in your past where you have no power anymore. Just remember.

Now tell them you forgive them and FEEL the forgiveness in your heart. *Feel* like you've forgiven them. You don't need special words or candles, just speak from your heart.

What Makes Me Happy?

If your life looks like an endless game of whack-a-mole, perhaps you need to find out what makes you happy?

After doing the meditations at the beginning of this chapter to clear your mind, think about the words "what makes me happy."

Think about your feelings and notice them. What lights you up? What brings a smile to your face? What do you NOT hate doing?

Then, quickly write down anything that comes to mind. Words, emotions, places, people, images ... don't think just write.

Do this for a few days in a row and then go back and read what you've written. I bet you'll see a common theme. If travel makes you happy, then working in a cubicle would not serve you. Perhaps you could look for a job that has you doing different things each day. If you see names of people popping up, then why not give them a call if they make you happy?

Listen, you need to BELIEVE in your happiness! You need to know that you absolutely positively deserve to be happy.

Now get up and go to a mirror and say to yourself "I deserve happiness." Say it out loud with feeling.

To be happy you must take action, even if it's only a small one. You need to start walking down that road.

You got this!

The Time Machine

As always, ground yourself before doing this exercise and call in your team of helpers.

Find a quiet place where no one will bother you.

Turn off your technology. Yes, I said turn it off again.

Now imagine you are in a time machine. Set the dial for a future where your current problem has been solved. It really doesn't matter how many days, weeks, months or years. Just set the intention that your problem or situation has been resolved in that reality.

How does it feel? What do you see around you? Who do you see? Imagine it using all your senses.

Now come back to the present.

What resources or actions can you take today that will move you toward that future? How can you make it work today?

Write down the first thoughts that fly into your mind.

You got this!

Life Assessment

Years ago, my friend Jackie shared an exercise with me where you go through each aspect of your business and look at what works, what doesn't work, what you could do better, what makes you happy, what you hate doing and the like.

So as I was writing this book, I thought it would be a good idea to do a review of your life as it is right now to see where the holes are and how you can make yourself feel better.

Ready? Let's go!

Your Physical Life

Your body

- How are you taking care of your physical body?

- What foods are you feeding it? Seriously, be honest. I promise not to tell anyone.
- Do you drink enough water?
- Are you moving your body or mostly sitting all day?
- What can you change to make yourself feel better? Again, be honest.

Your Home

- Do you like your home?
- Don't like your home? What can you change inside to make it feel better?
- What can you do right now to make moving to a new home a reality?

Your Job

- Do you like your job?
- Don't like your job? What change can you make? Job hunt? Get a promotion? Start a side hustle?

Your Family

- Do you have a positive/happy family life most of the time? NO ONE has one 100% of the time because life happens.
- No? What positive changes can you make within yourself to make it better?

Your Emotional Life

Your Feelings

- How are you feeling emotionally right now? If you are experiencing negative emotions such as anger or fear, try and move them to the positive. Think about what you are grateful for right now in this moment.

Take a look at what your feelings are towards your…

- Family
- Job/Career
- Health

What things do you do that make you happy?

What things do you do that make you uncomfortable? Do you have to do these things? If yes, how can you change your inner mindset to make it better? Don't have to do them? Then stop!

Your Mental Life

- Are you doing too many things at once?
- Do you have a hard time saying no to people?
- Is your day jam-packed?

Try and schedule some "love" time into your day… meaning stretches of time where you do things that you love. Taking a short walk. Meditate. Laugh. Play with your dog or cat. Color with your kids. Work on your hobby for 10 minutes. Do something you love that is NOT work related. Sing or dance to your favorite song!

Your Spiritual Life

I'm not talking about whether you practice a religion, I'm referring to your spirit. Your spiritual self. Some might wish to call this "their brain," and add it to the previous section. Fine with me!

Whatever you wish to call it, here's my question: what are you feeding it? It could be as simple as sitting still for a few minutes all by yourself. Not necessarily meditating, just being. (*Take a few deep breaths as you sit there.*)

- You could also meditate and make it a part of your daily routine.
- Take a walk outside and really try to live in the moment. Feel the grass and the sky. Look at the trees. Just "be" in nature and let your thoughts go where they want to.
- Try and avoid the energy vampires around you that are literally sucking the life out of you. Spend more time with the positive ones.

- Feeding your spirit, in my humble opinion, is reading (and watching) things that empower you and make you feel good. NOT things that make you feel guilty or imply what you should be doing.

CHAPTER 14

BIBLIOGRAPHY

Brown, Harriet. "How to Forgive Anyone—and Why Your Health Depends on It." http://www.oprah.com/oprahs-lifeclass/How-to-Forgive-Others-Health-Benefits-of-Forgiveness-FredLuskin#ixzz3ORMWJ7MI.

Holcombe, Madeline. "A Florida woman saw a crack forming in her condo and told herself, 'You have to run to save your life." https://www.cnn.com/2021/07/01/us/surfside-survivor-iliana-monteagudo/

Hudson, Clare. "5-Step Forgiveness Meditation Exercise." http://thoughtbrick.com/meditation/5-step-forgivenessmeditation-exercise/.

Maiden, Allison. "Are you Psychic? 7 Psychic Abilities You Might Have." https://thecarousel.com/wellness/psychic/

The Forgiveness Experiment. http://forgiveness.healingjourney.biz/forgiveness%20exp_004.htm.

Tiny Buddha. "How to Forgive Someone When It's Hard: 30 Tips to Let Go of Anger." http://tinybuddha.com/blog/how-to-forgivesomeone-when-its-hard-30-tips-to-let-go-of-anger/.

Vanzant, Iyanla. "3 Tools To Help You Forgive Someone." http://www.healyourlife.com/author-iyanla-vanzant/2013/12/wisdom/inspiration/3-ways-to-forgive.

Vanzant, Iyanla. "The Power of Forgiveness." http://live.huffingtonpost.com/r/segment/iyanla-vanzant-on-the-power-of-forgiveness/52b21cee2b8c2a24d1000284.

ABOUT THE AUTHOR

Katharine is a speaker/trainer, mentor, consultant, business intuitive, and three-time award-winning author. She is the author of six books including her award-winning inspirational book *"Rainbows and Banana Peels"*, her two-time award-winning book *"Going Above and Beyond"*, and her acclaimed book *"The Concierge Manual,"* now in its fifth edition.

ABOUT THE AUTHOR

Katharine has both been interviewed by and appeared on dozens of newspapers, magazines, radio and television shows from around the country including ABC News Nightline, CBS News, Good Morning America, MTV, Time Magazine, Money Magazine, Forbes, The New York Times and The Wall Street Journal to name a few.

A proud breast cancer survivor, Katharine was raised in New York City, earned a B.A. from Lake Forest College, and currently lives in North Carolina.

To read more about Katharine, or to reach out to her, please visit her at www.KatharineGiovanni.com or www.guidedtalk.com.

You GOT This!